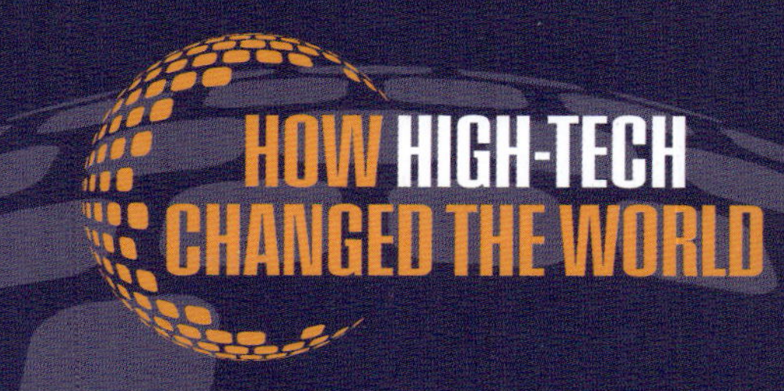

VOICE RECOGNITION

Published in 2025 by **Cheriton Children's Books**
1 Bank Drive West, Shrewsbury, Shropshire, SY3 9DJ

© Copyright 2025 Cheriton Children's Books

First Edition

Author: Kelly Roberts
Designer: Paul Myerscough
Editor: Jennifer Sanderson
Proofreader: Amy Strauss
Consultant: David Hawksett, BSc

Picture credits: Cover: Shutterstock/Boris Mayer (t), Shutterstock/Fizkes (c), Shutterstock/Panuwat Phimpha (r), Shutterstock/RossHelen (b). Inside: p4: Shutterstock/Fizkes, p5: Shutterstock/VesnaArt, p6: Shutterstock/Panuwat Phimpha, p7: Shutterstock/Zapp2Photo, p8: Shutterstock/PeopleImages.com/Yuri A, p9: Shutterstock/PrinceOfLove, p10: Shutterstock/Insta Photos, p11: Shutterstock/Raigvi, p12: Shutterstock/Tada Images, p13: Shutterstock/RossHelen, p14: Shutterstock/Fizkes, p15: Shutterstock/Everett Collection, p16b: Shutterstock/Sdx15, p16t: Shutterstock/Maxshot.PL, p17: Shutterstock/MIA Studio, p18: Shutterstock/Andrey Popov, p19: Shutterstock/Jittawit21, p20: Shutterstock/Fizkes, p21: Shutterstock/Urbanscape, p22: Shutterstock/Prostock Studio, p23: Shutterstock/Sdx15, p24: Shutterstock/Daniel M Ernst, p25: Shutterstock/Reddees, p26: Shutterstock/Aslysun, p27: Shutterstock/Fizkes, p28: Shutterstock/Dotshock, p29: Shutterstock/Kamazon Studio, p30: Shutterstock/Fizkes, p31bl: Shutterstock/Peace-loving, p31br: Shutterstock/Diego Thomazini, p32: Shutterstock/Piotr Swat, p33b: Shutterstock/Claudio Caridi, p33t: Shutterstock/Dean Drobot, p34: Shutterstock/Gorodenkoff, p35b: Shutterstock/PintoArt, p35t: Shutterstock/Kamil Zajaczkowski, p36: Shutterstock/Aarrows, p37: Shutterstock/Alpa Prod, p38: Shutterstock/Catwalker, p39: Shutterstock/AleksSafronov, p40: Shutterstock/Ground Picture, p41: Shutterstock/GoodAndy45, p42: Shutterstock/Andrey Popov, p43: Shutterstock/Zapp2Photo, p44: Shutterstock/Metamorworks, p45: Shutterstock/MikeDotta.

Printed in China

Please visit our website,
www.cheritonchildrensbooks.com
to see more of our high-quality books.

CONTENTS

CHAPTER 1

THE STORY OF VOICE RECOGNITION

Voice recognition is one of the wonders of modern technology. Whether you want to buy movie tickets, find the answers to a question that has been bugging you, or even write a letter by simply saying it into a microphone, voice recognition technology is there to help.

Transforming Sound

Voice recognition, which is sometimes called speech recognition, has many different uses. However, the basic principles behind each application remain more or less the same. The user speaks into a microphone on a device, such as a cell phone, and the computer in the device translates it to perform a specific task. This could be turning the spoken words into text, as if you were dictating a letter to somebody, opening a specific software application, such as a web browser, or answering a question, as Google Assistant and Siri do.

Smartphones, laptops, tablets, and even watches now come with voice recognition installed.

The Voice Recognition Revolution

The applications of voice recognition technology are almost endless. Voice recognition systems can be used in people's homes or offices to turn lights on and off. They can also be used to take credit card payments over the telephone. The systems can also assist people with disabilities in using a personal computer (PC). Voice recognition is revolutionizing our lives and will continue to do so for many years to come. In this book we'll discover more about the technology that makes voice recognition work. We'll also explore the history of voice recognition, how it has changed our world, and the brilliant scientists behind this incredible invention.

HOW HIGH-TECH CHANGED THE WORLD

In the past, when we wanted to buy movie or concert tickets, we would have to stand in a line, waiting for the box office to open. Then, voice recognition made it easier and we could buy tickets on the phone, without talking to a person. Today, using voice recognition is becoming more common. Smartphones, cars, and virtual assistants such as Siri and Alexa, can all respond to our commands, hugely simplifying our lives.

Know the Basics

The technology behind speech recognition systems is quite complicated. However, it can be simplified if the basic principles behind the systems are broken down into smaller steps. Whether you are calling an automated telephone service, such as the ones used by banks and companies that sell movie tickets, or using a speech recognition program on your computer, the technology behind the system is the same. First, the "user," or any person using the system, speaks into a microphone. The microphone will in some way be connected to a computer. This could be a desktop PC, a computer inside a smartphone, or a laptop. It could also be a computer at the other end of a telephone line or Internet connection.

Recording, Transforming, and Analyzing

While the user is speaking into the microphone, the voice recognition software will record the speech. This recording will then be turned into information that the computer can understand and analyze. The process of recording and analyzing can take anything from a few hundredths of a second to a few seconds, depending on how quick the computer is. Once the computer has analyzed what has been said, it can act on the instructions. This could be performing simple tasks or turning words into text in a word-processing document.

Speech recognition systems are used in smart cars. Scientists and computer experts have many different names for speech recognition systems. Sometimes, they are known as Automatic Speech Recognition (ASR) or Speech To Text (STT). Both names refer to the same technology.

HIGH-TECH HISTORY

In 1905, Karl F. Braun (1850–1918) first demonstrated a new technology called beamforming. Today, the latest cell phones use this technology to make their inbuilt microphones better than ever. Beamforming uses multiple microphones in different locations in the phone. These, along with complex algorithms, allow the phone to locate the direction of the user's voice. Then, the different microphones are adjusted to be more sensitive in the direction of the user's voice. Beamforming also helps with noise reduction by canceling out background sounds from all directions other than the user, and so has improved the accuracy of voice recognition systems.

Turning Speech into Data

Before the computer can act on any instructions, the voice recognition software inside the device must convert raw speech into data that the computer can understand. When people speak, they create vibrations in the air that can be heard as sounds. These vibrations are known as sound waves.

Long, Squiggly Lines

When the sound waves are recorded, they are analog sound waves. Sound waves look like long, squiggly lines. If you use a musicmaking or moviemaking program, such as Garageband or iMovie, you can see how sound waves look. Computers cannot understand analog sound waves.

Instead, they understand digital data, which is information recorded as a set of numbers. For speech recognition systems to work, the computers have to turn analog sound waves into digital data.

Going Digital

Speech recognition systems turn the sound waves into digital data using a device called an analog-to-digital converter (ADC). The ADC turns the sound into digital data by taking precise measurements of the wave at regular intervals—usually thousands of times a second. These measurements can then be turned into digital data. The digital data is analyzed using the system's speech recognition software.

The process of sampling, or digitally recording music, used by speech recognition systems is also used by music producers. They use sampling to record short segments of other people's music (often from vinyl records or CDs), which they can then use to create a new song.

HOW HIGH-TECH CHANGED THE WORLD

Professionals in the music industry use specialist equipment called digital audio workstations to create and edit music, including the use of samples. Once a sample of music is copied from its original format, such as a CD, the workstation stores it digitally in a library of samples. These can be accessed, altered, and added to the new piece of music. Today, home users can buy software that can make a PC act like a virtual digital audio workstation. This means that anyone can create music with samples, not just the professionals. And with social media platforms on which to share their music, being a chart-topping musician has never been simpler.

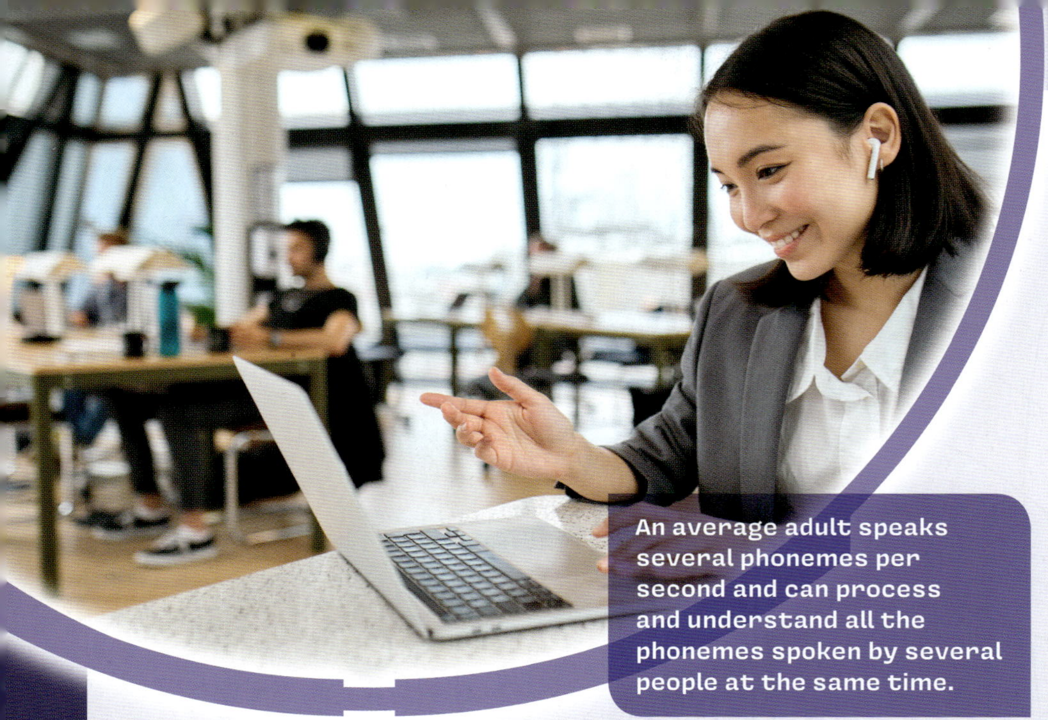

An average adult speaks several phonemes per second and can process and understand all the phonemes spoken by several people at the same time.

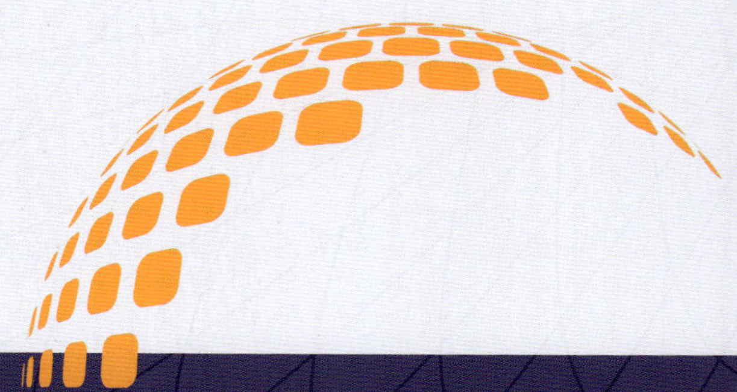

Matching Sounds

The process used by speech recognition systems to analyze the digital data converted from sound waves is incredibly complicated. It involves matching the data created with examples stored in the speech recognition software. The software must match the data to the digital representations of sounds, which are known as phonemes.

Understanding Phonemes

Phonemes are the smallest element of a spoken language. They are the building blocks of speech. All words, when spoken, regardless of the language, are made up of a combination of different phonemes. To recreate or to understand what has been spoken, the speech recognition system must put these phonemes in the correct order, in which they can be recognized.

Making Words

Putting the phonemes in the correct order to make meaningful words is a complex task. This is because many words use similar combinations of phonemes, or the words sound similar but mean different things. Today's speech recognition systems not only order these phonemes but they also have to try to match them with the words stored in the system's software. To match the phonemes, scientists have invented a number of algorithms. The algorithms help the system examine each phoneme in context with any other phonemes around it. By doing this, the system can make an accurate decision about exactly what was said.

Many Phonemes

There are roughly 40 different phonemes in the English language. Some other languages, such as Mandarin and Japanese, have many, many more. Each phoneme represents a particular sound people use when speaking. Even a simple word such as "and" uses three phonemes: "a," "n," and "d." Try saying it out loud!

HIGH-TECH STARS WHO CHANGED THE WORLD

JACK KILBY

Voice recognition would not be possible without the integrated circuit (IC). The IC was invented by Jack Kilby (1923–2005) in 1958. ICs used miniaturized components, such as resistors, capacitors, and transistors, on a single semiconductor chip, allowing for the development of the ADC. ADCs convert analog signals, such as sound levels, into data. They can also measure other qualities of a sound, including tone. This meant that simple phonemes could be identified. Another engineer named Robert Noyce (1927–1990) independently invented the IC around the same time. Kilby and Noyce shared the 2000 Nobel Prize in Physics for their work.

an IC

Using Algorithms

The complicated algorithms used by speech recognition systems figure out the probability that the sounds that have been identified are a specific word, phrase, or sentence. There is a limited number of phonemes in the English language, but more than 300,000 words in the Merriam-Webster dictionary. Algorithms are used to sort through all the phonemes and words to accurately identify the words that were spoken by the user of the voice recognition device. To do this, scientists developed an algorithm called the hidden Markov model. It second-guesses the user and, using a detective-style process of deduction, figures out what was said.

The Hidden Markov Model

In the hidden Markov model, each phoneme is treated like a link in a chain, with the completed chain making up a word. Each link is cross-referenced with the list of phonemes and words stored in the system's dictionary. To complete the chain, the system must figure out exactly which of the links come next. To help out the system, each likely link is given a "probability score," based on the possibility that it will come next (the higher the score, the more likely it is). By using this process of deduction, the algorithm will identify the right word more often than not.

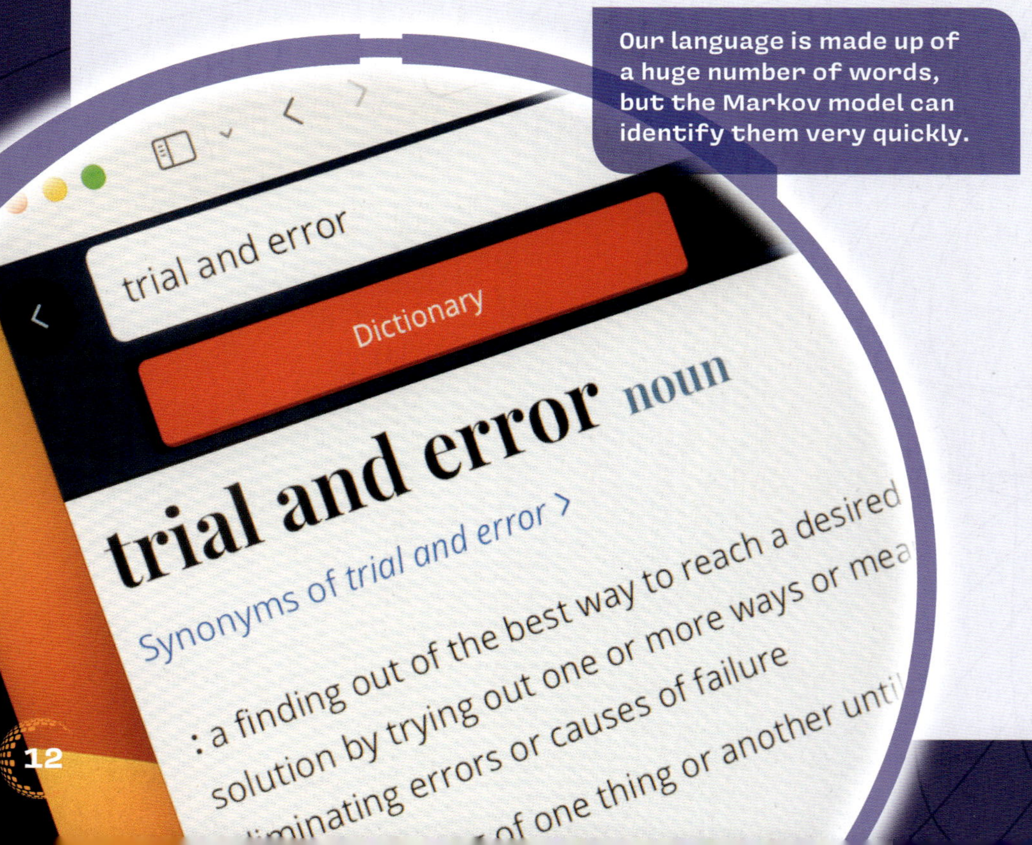

HIGH-TECH STARS WHO CHANGED THE WORLD

LEONARD ESAU BAUM

Leonard Esau Baum (1931–2017) was an American mathematician. In the late 1960s, while working at the Communications Research Division of the Institute for Defense Analyses (IDA) in Princeton, Baum and his colleague Lloyd R. Welch (1927–2023) invented the Baum–Welch algorithm. It uses two steps—expectation and maximization—to train a hidden Markov model to recognize phonemes in a spoken voice. The algorithm lets voice recognition software adjust its expectations of what it will hear based on what it has already heard. The algorithm made voice recognition more accurate, especially in the case of normal continuous speech. The Baum–Welch algorithm also reduced the amount of computing power needed for voice recognition, which was an important advancement at a time when computers were still basic.

Today's voice recognition systems are capable of recording and sampling speech at incredibly high speeds. Most telephone-based speech recognition systems now have a sample rate that allows them to record 8,000 samples each second!

The Limitations

Thanks to advances in algorithms and more powerful PCs, speech recognition systems are much more accurate than they once were. However, there are still issues with many systems that software developers have yet to fully solve.

Dealing with Background Noise

Using the hidden Markov model guarantees quite accurate results most of the time. However, there are some flaws in it. If the user's microphone or telephone receiver picks up a lot of background noise—for example, if it is being used in a busy office or at a railroad station—the speech recognition system may struggle to accurately identify each individual sound.

Speak Slowly!

Speech recognition systems also work better when people speak slowly and clearly. If you talk quickly, and "run" words into each other (for example, saying "y'all" instead of "you all"), the system will find it hard to figure out what you are saying.

Slang and Accents Are Problematic

Speech recognition systems are also easily confused by slang words, as these may not appear in the dictionary. Regional accents can also be problematic. People in different parts of the same country often say the same things differently, and this can confuse speech recognition programs. This is why people often complain about automated telephone services that ask them to repeat words. The system does this because it cannot understand what the speaker said.

HIGH-TECH HISTORY

Thomas Edison (1847–1931) invented the phonograph in the late nineteenth century. The phonograph was the first-ever device that could record and play back sound. Edison thought it would be mostly useful as a dictation machine in offices. Early versions used a stylus to etch sound into a spiral groove on a wax cylinder or disk. Improvements gradually transformed the phonograph into the turntable record player, which is still used by many to listen to music. Audio recording was a critical step in the rise of voice recognition.

Thomas Edison

CHAPTER 2

CONVERTING SOUND WAVES

Today's high-tech speech recognition systems began in the nineteenth century. During this time, it was discovered that sound waves could be converted into electrical signals. However, it was another 60 years before anybody attempted to turn sound into digital data.

In the 1970s, computers were mostly used only by the government, military, scientific institutes, and businesses.

Making Audrey

The big breakthrough in voice recognition came in 1952, when a company called Bell Laboratories successfully invented a computer that could recognize basic speech. The Automatic Digit Recognizer, or "Audrey" as it was known, was able to understand numbers (zero and one to nine). However, the speaker had to talk slowly and clearly, leaving large gaps between each number.

HIGH-TECH HISTORY

In 1961, the computer company IBM developed a computer that not only recognized speech but could also perform basic math. The computer was the approximate size and shape of a normal shoebox, and so it became known as The Shoebox. It could recognize numbers from 0 to 10, as well as commands such as "plus," "minus," and "total." Ten small lights on its side represented the numbers 0 to 9, and they would light up when the number was spoken into a mouthpiece and converted into electrical signals by the machine. The Shoebox was an experimental prototype used to demonstrate futuristic voice recognition technology, showing the world what could be possible.

Advancing the Tech

In the early 1970s, the technology really began to move forward. Several cutting-edge systems were invented that understood a greater number of words as well as numbers. However, as the computers of the 1970s were neither very powerful nor advanced, the speech recognition systems were of limited use.

The Government Invests

The US government saw the potential of speech recognition, though, and in early 1971, it began to invest money into the Department of Defense's DARPA Speech Understanding Research (SUR) program. The program ran for 5 years and managed to develop a system called Harpy, which understood 1,011 words —roughly the same as an average 3-year-old. As a result of this research, speech recognition systems were on sale by the late 1970s. They were not cheap, though, and the best system could cost $100,000!

The Harpy voice recognition system could understand as many words as a young child, which was advanced for the 1970s tech.

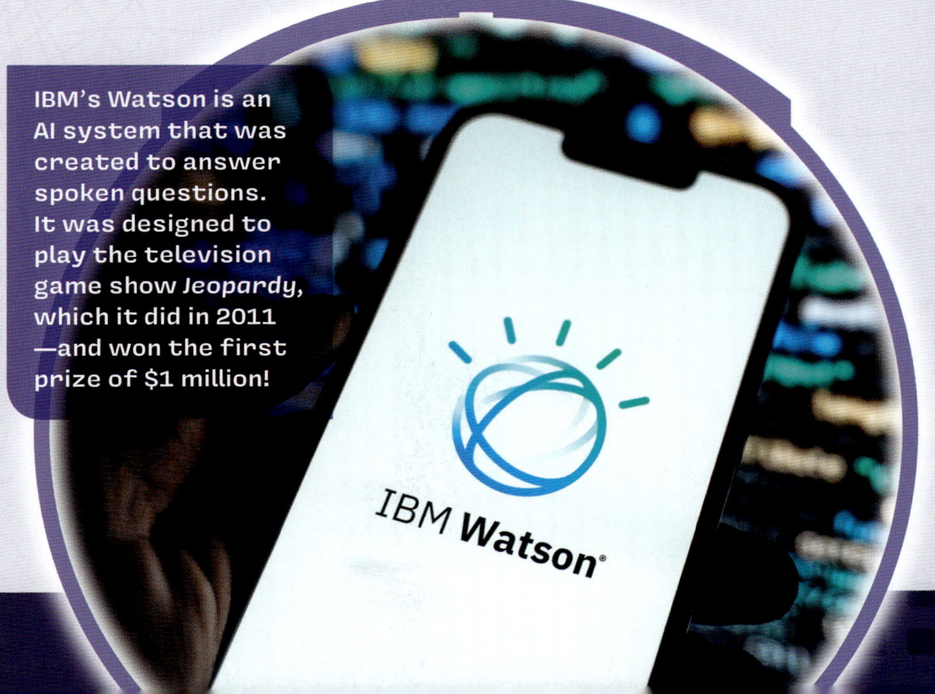

IBM's Watson is an AI system that was created to answer spoken questions. It was designed to play the television game show *Jeopardy*, which it did in 2011 —and won the first prize of $1 million!

The Drawbacks

Early voice recognition systems worked but they were limited in what they could do. They could recognize only a limited number of words and they were based on known rules of the English language, such as grammar. For the systems to work, words and sentences had to be spoken slowly and they had to abide by the rules.

Making Progress

The invention of the hidden Markov model algorithm in the early 1960s (see page 13) changed speech recognition systems forever. In the early 1980s, computer programmer Jim Baker created a way of using the hidden Markov model for speech recognition. This revolutionized speech recognition by considering the probability that certain sequences of sounds made up specific words.

Julie the Doll

The first mass-market use of speech recognition technology was not computer software. It was, in fact, a pioneering children's doll named Julie. Launched in 1987, Julie featured speech recognition technology that allowed users to teach her words. Julie also responded to questions. She even giggled if you tickled her!

Unlike today's systems that even younger children can use, the first voice recognition systems were limited because the language used had to follow traditional grammar rules.

Chatbots are designed to make the voice recognition experience more user-friendly, and will become much more intelligent in future devices.

Selling to Professionals

During the 1980s, expensive speech recognition systems were sold to companies for use in the healthcare and legal professions. While advanced for the time, they were nowhere near as advanced as the systems we know and use today. One of the systems' biggest drawbacks was the computers used at the time. These were basic and expensive. At this time, few people owned home computers, and the systems were unsuitable for them anyway.

HIGH-TECH HISTORY

In the 1960s, Japanese computer scientists developed their own voice recognition machines. Tokyo's Radio Research Lab created one that could recognize only vowels. Kyoto University built a machine that could understand 100 Japanese phonemes. Technology company NEC also made its own device that could recognize spoken numbers. NEC tested the invention by giving it 1,000 digits spoken by 20 different men. The company's voice recognition machine achieved a 99.7 percent success rate, which was very impressive for the 1960s.

The Computer Age

During the 1990s, faster, cheaper computers and better-quality voice recognition systems combined to bring speech recognition software to people's homes. The move toward making speech recognition part of our everyday lives had begun.

A New System

In 1990, Jim Baker and his wife Janet Baker, launched a new voice recognition system called DragonDictate. It was the first speech recognition tool aimed at home computer users. But, at $9,000 it was still too expensive for most people to afford, so the Bakers spent the next seven years perfecting their system, and in 1997, they replaced it with a new system called Dragon NaturallySpeaking.

Costing around $700, Dragon NaturallySpeaking had suddenly made voice recognition software much more affordable. The system recognized continuous speech and featured a dictionary of around 10,000 words. Users could speak naturally, at around 100 words a minute, and the system would keep up. However, they had to spend 45 minutes "training" it to understand them before they could use it.

On the Phone

The 1990s saw the development of another great speech recognition system that is widely used today. The automated telephone system uses speech recognition technology in a different way. The users dial a number, and a recorded voice on the other end of the line asks a series of questions. The system recognizes the answers and reacts accordingly.

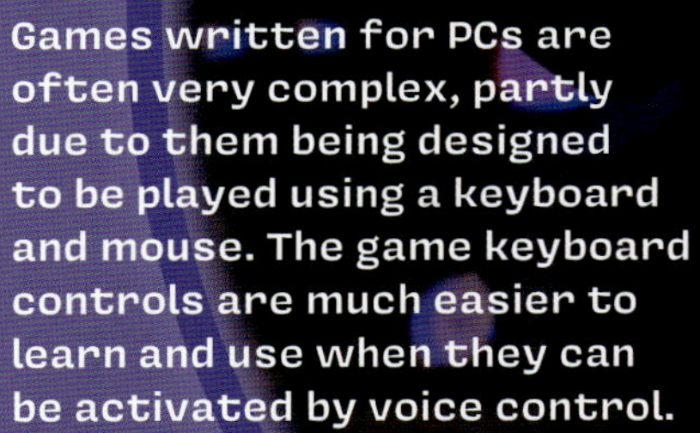

Dial in to Val

The first ever "dial-in interactive voice recognition system," or automated telephone service, was launched in 1996. It was based on a system called VAL, which was capable of listening to what you said, understanding different options, and giving you information based on your answers to simple questions.

HOW HIGH-TECH CHANGED THE WORLD

In the late 1990s, most people relied on a dial-up connection to access the Internet. It was impossible to be online and make a phone call at the same time. Online gaming was gaining popularity and gamers could play together using dial-up but they could not talk to each other. Then in 2000, Microsoft released its Game Voice device, which allowed gaming and voice chat over dial-up when connected to a PC. Game Voice was also designed for voice recognition and made it possible to play certain games using voice commands. Game Voice helped drive the development of voice recognition for entertainment, as well as making gaming more accessible to people with physical disabilities.

Bringing the Tech to You

Since the turn of the century, voice recognition technology has really advanced. Today, what was once incredibly expensive software is available to everyone. There are voice recognition systems built into smartphones, laptops, and home computers to make this technology a part of our everyday lives.

Building It In

As computer speech recognition programs have become more accurate and faster—and people's home computers have become more powerful—manufacturers have started building speech recognition software into their systems. Since 2005, Microsoft and Apple Computers have included speech recognition and voice commands in their operating systems. Operating systems, such as Windows and macOS, are the framework around which all home computers are built. Using speech recognition means that people can tell their computers what to do—for example, opening and closing activity windows or changing settings such as brightness and volume.

Hey, Siri!

The development of smartphones, such as Apple's iPhone, brought about the next big advance in speech recognition technology. Today, all smartphones come with software programs based on voice recognition technology. One of the most famous of these is the iPhone's "Siri" program, which will try to answer almost any question.

Voice Search

In 2008, the Google search engine allowed users to do an Internet search by speaking into their computer cr cell phone instead of keying in the information. This system, called Google Voice Search, soon became so popular that in 2011, it was turned into a smartphone app.

HIGH-TECH STARS WHO CHANGED THE WORLD

ADAM CHEYER

Adam Cheyer is the brilliant computer scientist behind Apple's Siri. In 2007, he was working on a military-funded AI project at SRI International, a scientific research institute in California, when he, Dag Kittlaus, and Tom Gruber founded Siri Inc. This was based on their military work to create an AI assistant for soldiers. Three years later, Siri Inc was bought by Apple, and the company began integrating it into its operating systems.

Siri was originally designed for military use.

CHAPTER 3

TODAY'S SYSTEMS

There are two main types of voice recognition system used today—those designed for a large number of users and those meant to be used by only one or two people. Each system has different strengths and weaknesses, and each is used for a specific purpose.

Simple but Smart

The most popular speech recognition systems are those designed for use by a large number of people. These are the systems used by automated telephone services and apps, such as Google Voice Search. For this type of voice system to work properly, it has to be set up to recognize only a few common words and commands. However, these systems can only recognize certain accents and speech patterns.

Keeping It Short and Sweet

When you call an automated telephone service, such as one used to book movie or concert tickets, the service sometimes has difficulty understanding or recognizing what you say. If this is the case, a voice may ask you to repeat what you have said. This type of system is no use to those who want to speak a lot, as it really only understands numbers and very basic words such as "yes," "no," and names of places or popular movies.

There are around 6,500 languages in use today, all of which have variations in accent. Voice recognition software cannot yet understand and translate all of them.

Dealing with Accents

The companies that operate automated voice recognition systems decide the words, commands, and numbers it will recognize, based on the nature of their business. They then train the system to recognize the many ways people from different areas say these words, commands, and numbers. By doing this, the system should be able to cope with different regional or national accents.

HOW HIGH-TECH CHANGED THE WORLD

Google Voice Search was launched by Google in 2012. It was intended to give users a hands-free way of searching the World Wide Web (WWW) using their search engine. As Google developed and released more apps, it began building voice commands into their basic functions. Google maps could be controlled by voice alone, including the ability to set destinations. Users could also use the note-taking app Google Keep as a voice dictation app. Google Voice Search gradually evolved into today's Google Assistant, which can translate more than 100 languages.

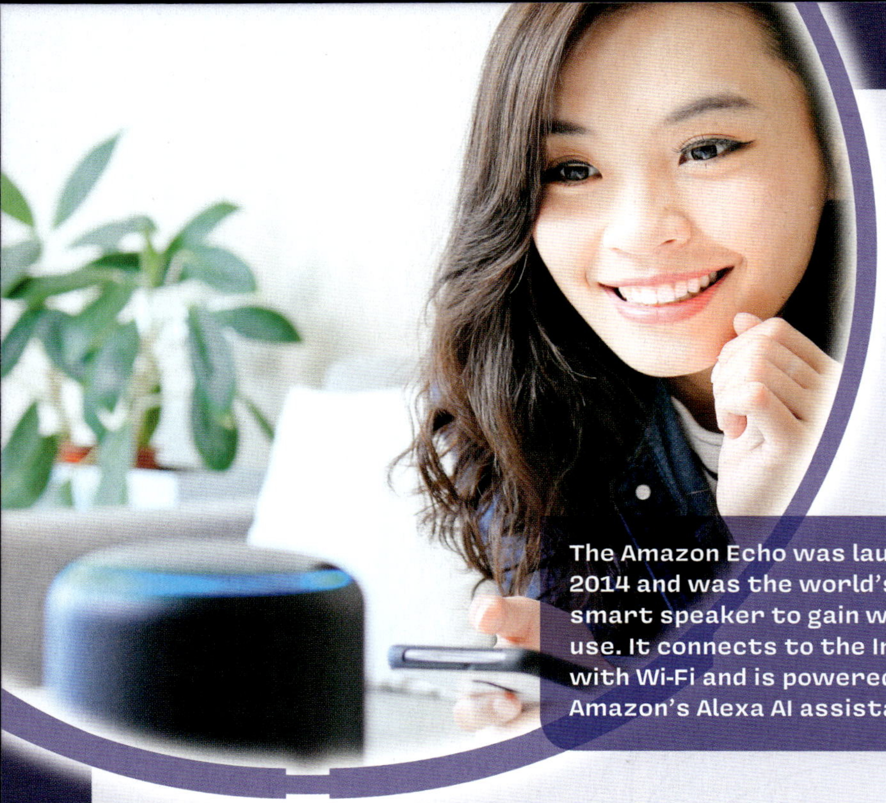

The Amazon Echo was launched in 2014 and was the world's first smart speaker to gain widespread use. It connects to the Internet with Wi-Fi and is powered by Amazon's Alexa AI assistant.

Only for a Few

The second type of voice recognition system is designed for use by a very limited number of users, perhaps just one or two people. It is this type of system that experts have been perfecting since the 1980s. Limited-user voice recognition systems are far more accurate than the systems used in automated telephone services. Typically, they can get between 85 and 90 percent of words right. They are also able to recognize many more words—60,000 or more. One of the most well-known programs that uses this type of system is Dragon NaturallySpeaking, the pioneering speech recognition program (see page 20).

Being Trained

As their name suggests, limited-user systems work well if they are used by a very small number of people. This is because the systems become familiar with the way these people speak and pronounce particular words. However, there is a catch to using the systems—for them to perform well, each user must first train the software to recognize their speech patterns.

Quick and Easy

Training a speech recognition system on your computer is surprisingly easy. After a quick microphone test, the system will then ask you to read out a short passage of text displayed on your computer screen. This is so that it can begin to learn your speech patterns and how you say certain key words.

HIGH-TECH HISTORY

In 2007 Google launched GOOG-411 in North America as a speech recognition telephone directory search service. Upon calling, users would say the state and city of a business and could then search using the name or type of the business they were looking for. GOOG-411 operated until 2010 and allowed Google to collect a large database of spoken phonemes from the recorded voices of all of its users. This helped Google develop and improve its voice recognition technology.

Using voice recognition to take notes and write emails can be faster than typing and can also allow users to create text that feels less formal. Dictation software will even add the punctuation.

VOICE RECOGNITION SYSTEMS IN ACTION

Today, voice recognition technology has many different uses. Some of these uses we encounter in our day-to-day lives but there are many other applications of voice recognition that you are probably not aware of. Speech recognition in automated telephone services is becoming increasingly common. Today, these systems are used mostly by companies that have call centers and have to deal with many people on a daily basis. These organizations include banks and cable television operators as well as box offices and electricity companies.

Saving Money

Although speech recognition systems are expensive to buy and set up, in the long run, the companies save money. They do not have to employ as many people to answer their phones.

The companies can also use the system to direct each call to the right department. This is often done using a set of prerecorded questions, the answers to which help the system forward the call to the correct part of the organization.

One major benefit of having AI answer calls is that just one computer can deal with multiple calls at once. Traditional call centers are less environmentally friendly because each human operator needs their own computer workstation.

Caller Identification

Automated telephone services are also good for companies, such as banks, which have a lot of customers and deal with sensitive information. These companies can use the automated service to identify the caller, asking for passwords and other key identifying details, before allowing the customer to speak to a representative.

When It's Frustrating

Automated telephone services that use speech recognition do not have a good reputation. Many people find them very annoying as they seem to fail regularly. When this happens, it is often because the system does not understand what the person has said. People with strong regional accents or foreigners have the most problems with these systems.

Since 2017, voice biometrics have been used to recognize the voice of an individual. This new voice recognition technology is used by banks and other industries where sensitive data is held. The customer activates this service during a telephone call by repeating a phrase several times. The automated phone system then measures more than 100 different qualities of that person's voice so that the customer can log into their account using their voice, with no need for a password. Voice biometrics make it much harder to steal a person's login details, keeping data safe and secure.

Everyone's voice pattern is unique, making it perfect for biometric recognition.

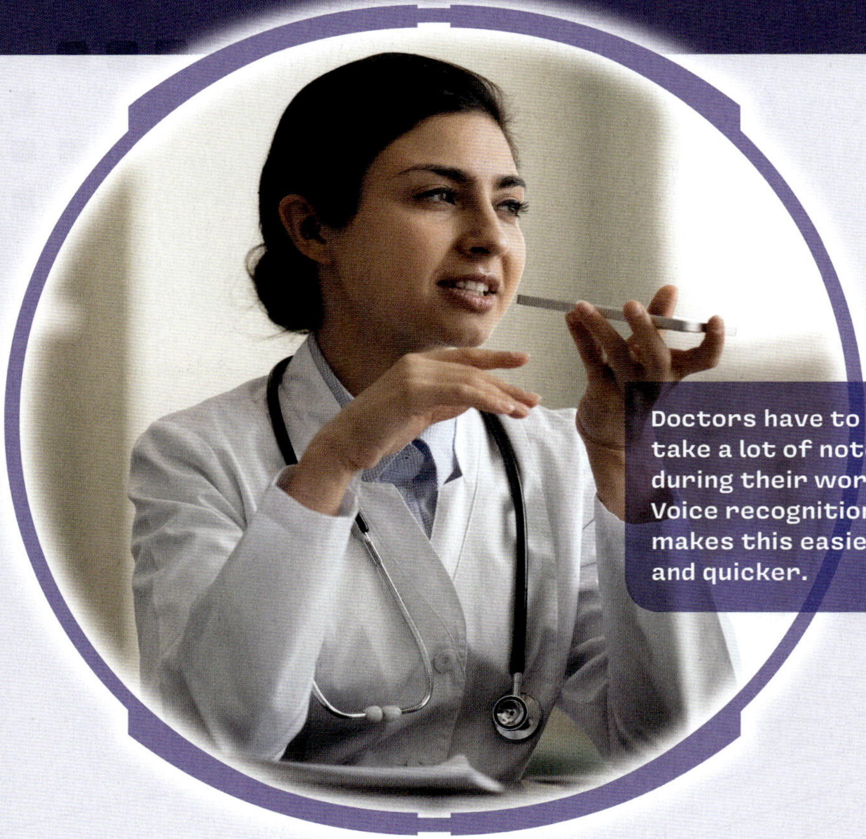

Doctors have to take a lot of notes during their work. Voice recognition makes this easier and quicker.

Speech Recognition in the Workplace

Speech recognition technology has transformed the working world. Today, many people use speech recognition systems in their workplace, and in some areas, it is becoming as essential as a telephone and computer.

Dictation Made Easy

When using speech recognition technology first became popular during the late 1990s and early 2000s, makers of voice recognition software aimed their products at businesses. Today, many companies run systems aimed at limited users. Instead of dictating letters to a secretary or assistant, who would write them down, many managers now choose to dictate their letters and reports into a computer running speech recognition software. The software turns their spoken words into text, so they can write and send letters quickly.

Quicker than Typing

Using speech recognition software to dictate notes and letters has become a popular way of working across a range of industries but is arguably most popular in the legal and healthcare professions. It saves lawyers, attorneys, and doctors valuable time. Speech recognition options built into computer operating systems have also become increasingly popular with those who struggle to type. Using voice commands, they can control their computers without having to touch the mouse, trackpad, or keyboard.

Different Systems

Doctors currently have a choice between two voice recognition systems: front end and back end speech recognition. Front end systems display the words, as you say them, onto a computer screen. Back end systems, on the other hand, analyze previously made recordings and email the analyzed document to the doctor a few hours later.

In 2014, Microsoft unveiled Cortana as a virtual assistant for its Windows operating system. Cortana used voice recognition to answer questions from the user and could set reminders, do a web search, and control the computer's basic functions, such as shutting it down, with a verbal command. In 2023, Cortana was replaced with Microsoft Copilot, which is an AI chatbot. Copilot can do many things: it can even write songs. Soon, Copilot will have its own button on keyboards, making it even more accessible.

Cortana was named for the AI character in the Xbox video game Halo.

Mobile Voice Recognition

Today, many of us carry around tiny speech recognition systems in our pockets. Thanks to the integration of voice commands into the operating systems of smartphones, you can now use these phones without ever touching the screen or keypad.

Giving the Command

There are two popular operating systems used in smartphones. They are Google's Android and Apple's iOS. Both operating systems respond to voice commands. They work in a similar way, too. You activate them by saying a "wake" phrase, such as "Hey, Siri" or "Hey, Google." You then need to tell your phone what to do by saying commands, such as "Phone Mom," or "Search the Internet." You can even ask your phone to search nearby for places to eat, or to play a particular song or album.

Talking to Siri

Siri is at the cutting edge of speech recognition technology. Not only does Siri respond to simple commands, but it also learns about you by remembering what you search for on the WWW and what music you listen to. It cross-references the way you speak with a huge bank of accents and speech patterns stored in its memory. The more you use Siri, the better it understands you.

Silly Siri!

Siri is quite revolutionary. It does not just respond to simple commands, such as "Play music," but it will also try to answer simple questions, speak back to you, and, if you ask silly questions, give you silly answers—try it for yourself!

Using your phone hands-free lets you make and receive calls when you would not normally be able to, such as while cooking.

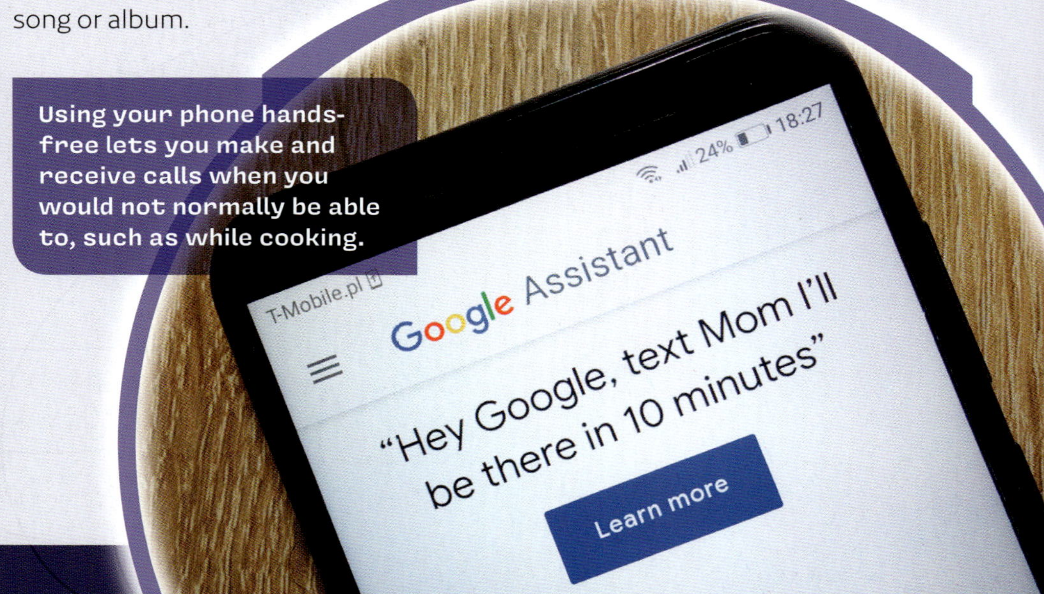

HOW HIGH-TECH CHANGED THE WORLD

In 2014, 20 years after it began as an online book store, Amazon launched its own virtual personal assistant in its Amazon Echo smart speaker. Alexa, like the Google and Apple assistants, responds to a wake word, so it is always listening out for its name. Manufacturers of smart home gadgets soon began contacting Amazon as they wanted their own devices to be linked to and controlled by Alexa. Today, Amazon's assistant can control hundreds of smart home devices, such as lighting, heating, security systems, as well as home computers. Alexa can also be used on a smart watch.

Air traffic controllers are rigorously trained by computer software and voice recognition to cope with any situation or emergency. The smallest mistake by controllers can lead to disaster.

Voice Recognition in Training

Speech recognition systems are widely used in the workplace in many different ways. One very important way is in the training of people to do difficult and demanding jobs, such as being an air traffic controller, which is one of the most difficult and stressful jobs. It is an air traffic controller's responsibility to ensure that airplanes not only take off and land safely at airports, but that they also take the correct route through the skies. Training new air traffic controllers takes a lot of time and is very difficult. In the past, it required a lot of input from experienced controllers, who would test out their recruits' skills by pretending to be a pilot trying to land a plane.

Using Voice Recognition

Today, experienced air traffic controllers no longer have to train the junior controllers in the same way. Instead, a trainee air traffic controller goes into a simulation booth and is given a specific task to perform, such as safely guiding a plane into an airport. In a real-life situation, the controller would speak to a pilot. In this training situation, there is no pilot—just a computer loaded with prerecorded speech and a voice recognition system. The computerized pilot responds to what the trainee controller says. Air traffic controllers are supposed to use only about 150 standard phrases when talking to pilots. However, the leading training systems recognize more than 500,000 different phrases.

Learning a New Language

Speech recognition systems are now being used to help people learn foreign languages. Many popular computer assisted language learning (CALL) programs include speech recognition technology to help people learn without the need for a human language teacher.

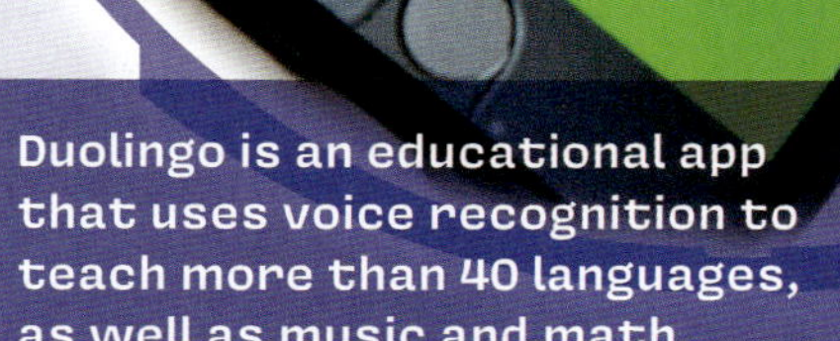

Duolingo is an educational app that uses voice recognition to teach more than 40 languages, as well as music and math.

HOW HIGH-TECH CHANGED THE WORLD

Dragon Medical One is designed to help doctors deal with patients more efficiently. It allows for direct voice dictation into medical notes with a 99 percent accuracy, with no voice training and using any accent. There are more than 16,000 medical terms used by doctors, not including the names for specific drugs. Dragon Medical One uses cloud-based AI to understand all of these terms so that a doctor can save time by dictating notes and inputting data, allowing them to spend more time with patients.

Military Uses

Ever since the US Department of Defense (DoD) invested huge amounts of money in research into speech recognition in the 1970s, the military has seen the potential in voice commands and controls. Over the last few years, air forces around the world have started to use voice recognition systems in fighter jets. This makes a lot of sense as fighter pilots have a lot to do in combat. They must fly a plane at high speed and at the same time, they must communicate with their commanders and, sometimes, fire missiles or other weapons at enemy planes.

US Air Forces

The US Air Force has adopted speech recognition systems and installed them within planes. A number of F-35 fighter jets used by the Air Force now have speech recognition voice control systems. Pilots can use the system to set radio frequencies, turn on the autopilot system, set steering controls, and change the information displayed on the screens in the cockpit.

In the Air

Other air forces around the world have also developed speech recognition systems in some of their planes. The Eurofighter Typhoon jet, which is used by several European air forces, has a system that requires each pilot to create their own "template." This template helps the pilot train the plane's system to understand how the pilot speaks. The British Royal Air Force (RAF) says that training and using the system this way has helped lighten the load on pilots, allowing them to concentrate on flying their planes.

In Helicopters

The US Air Force is investing a lot of money in creating a voice recognition system that can be used in the cockpits of helicopters. This is a great development in voice recognition because noise can reduce the effectiveness of voice control systems, and a helicopter cockpit is noisy.

In 2016, Garmin introduced its Telligence voice command system for civilian aircraft. Once activated with a push-to-talk button, pilots can give instructions and ask the plane's navigation computer questions. They can use simple phrases to check the weather at their destination, create flight path waypoints, tune in to an airport's radio channel, and control many other functions. Today's new pilots are already familiar with AI assistants with voice control, so manufacturers are building more into their aircraft computers. Some experts believe this is a critical step toward commercial jets being fully-autonomous by 2050.

Developing Robots

It might sound like something from a science-fiction movie, but scientists have recently invented robots with human characteristics—including the ability to recognize and respond to different voices. These robots are called androids.

Honda's ASIMO

In 2000, Japanese company Honda unveiled its most humanlike robot yet: ASIMO (an acronym for Advanced Step in Innovative Mobility). Now featured at the Miraikan museum in Tokyo, Japan, ASIMO walks and moves like a person. More amazingly, ASIMO can recognize faces, move out of the way when somebody approaches, and can carry out tasks such as moving objects. ASIMO can even run, albeit slowly.

Like a Person

Honda's ASIMO and other androids have inbuilt speech recognition technology, which means they can respond to voice commands. They turn their head toward the direction of the person speaking (or an unusual sound, such as breaking glass or a heavy object hitting the ground), and can respond to simple questions. Many speech recognition systems can recognize a few different voices and respond accordingly. As well as recognizing voices, they also learn names. This means that when you talk to an android, it can address you by your name—like it knows you!

ASIMO made its last appearance in 2022. Now that it is retired, Honda scientists are using what they have learned by developing it to create more practical uses for robots.

Ford SYNC

Many of the latest cars feature speech recognition technology. Products such as Ford SYNC, found in modern Ford cars, allow drivers to make phone calls, play music, and control the car's satellite navigation system. The latest versions also let drivers control the sunroof, windows, wipers, and air conditioning with voice commands.

HIGH-TECH STARS WHO CHANGED THE WORLD

TOSHITADO DOI

In the 1990s, Toshitado Doi led the team at Sony that created the revolutionary AIBO toy. Doi designed a pet robotic dog called AIBO, which went on sale in 1999. The dog can do tricks and later versions have simple vision that can track and follow a small ball. AIBO has voice recognition and can understand and act on more than 50 voice commands such as "Sit down," "Kick the ball," and "Take a picture." Thanks to AIBO, Toshitado Doi brought modern voice recognition to the world of entertainment.

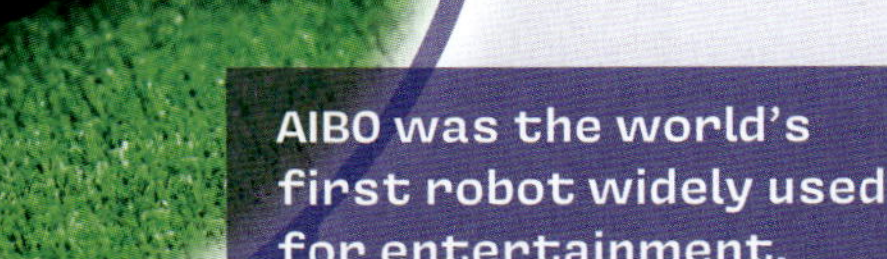

AIBO was the world's first robot widely used for entertainment.

CHAPTER 5

DEVELOPING NEW TECH

Voice recognition technology has advanced a great deal in the last 25 years. Given the speed of these developments, it is likely that new speech recognition technology will be even more sophisticated in the coming years. So what can we expect from voice recognition technology in the future?

Translation Experts

There are many skilled translators in the world. These people specialize in translating from one language into another. Most professional translators know about four or five languages. However, experts say that there are around 6,500 different languages spoken in the world today. Imagine being able to carry around a small, computerized device that is able to understand any one of these languages, and translate it into your chosen language. Scientists think that one day, voice recognition technology will make this possible. In fact, research has already begun to create what scientists call the "universal translator." To create a device that can instantly translate between all the different languages spoken around the world will take computer scientists many years.

Small Steps

The universal translator may still be a dream but there are products available that can translate between different spoken languages. The WorldPenScan Go can recognize 112 spoken languages. If you speak into it, it can instantly translate and play back your words in any of those languages. It allows people to hold conversations even if they do not speak the same language.

One human translator could never learn all of the world's many different languages.

Helping Soldiers

During the Iraq War (2003–2011) the US Army developed a two-way translator called TRANSTAC. TRANSTAC used speech recognition to understand both Arabic and English, as well as Farsi, a language spoken in Iran and its neighboring countries. TRANSTAC was able to translate from one language into the other, which proved vital to soldiers based in Iraq, and later, Afghanistan during the Afghanistan War (2001–2021).

Spying on international calls has always been a tool of intelligence agencies, including the US National Security Agency (NSA). In the past, this needed actual agents to listen in on recorded calls but with the huge scale of global communications, there were not enough ears. Today, thanks to voice recognition software, the NSA can record any phone call and automatically turn the voice into text documents, which can be analyzed by NSA agents to look for potential threats.

Other Uses for Voice Recognition

Although the universal translator is still some way off from becoming an everyday device, it is not the only avenue being explored by scientists and software engineers. They think that in the future, there will be many other uses for voice recognition technology in our daily lives.

In Homes

Computer scientists believe that one day, our homes could come with speech recognition technology built into different parts of the house. It is already possible to have light switches that respond to voice commands. In the future, you will be able to lock and unlock your doors and windows using your own voice. These voice command systems could also double as security systems by responding only to the speech patterns and exact sound of a specific speaker.

Understanding Humans

Some computer scientists also believe that speech recognition will play a key role in developing computers, robots, and other devices with true AI. At present, most speech recognition systems can recognize words, phrases, and speech patterns, and act on them. However, the systems still do not understand what the user is saying. A device or computer with true AI would understand everything a person says. They will be able to think for themselves, just like people do. Although it sounds far-fetched, it is thought that the technology will be available sooner rather than later, possibly in just a few years.

Homes are becoming smarter, with more and more device types being connected to home Wi-Fi networks that can be controlled with voice recognition. Combined, these devices have become known as the Internet of Things (IoT).

HIGH-TECH HISTORY

The idea of a universal translator was used in a 1945 science-fiction novel titled *First Contact*. However, it was Gene Roddenberry (1921–1991) who made the idea popular in the late 1960s. Gene created the original *Star Trek* television show and a universal translator was one of the futuristic tools used by the show's characters. It worked instantaneously for all languages, including those of aliens encountered for the first time. *Star Trek* also had personal communicators that looked like flip phones, 30 years before we had them in reality. Wireless headsets, tablet computers, and voice recognition AI assistants were also predicted by the show.

Monitoring and Translating

In the mid-2000s, the US government funded a project called Global Autonomous Language Exploitation (GALE). The scientists on the project developed systems that monitor broadcasts in Mandarin and Arabic, before translating them into English. The scientists behind GALE hope that in the future, they will be able to do the same with all languages.

In the future, robot assistants will be capable of carrying out household tasks, all controlled by voice.

A HIGH-TECH FUTURE

Voice recognition systems have come a long way in a short space of time. They have developed from simple computers that understand a few numbers to amazing devices capable of translating between many different languages. And, in the process, they have changed our lives forever.

Real Life

Only recently, television viewers and movie audiences marveled at the speech recognition systems imagined by the writers of *Star Trek*. Now, similar systems are part of our everyday lives. Consider your own life. You or someone in your house almost certainly owns a smartphone that can be controlled using voice commands. You may have used an automated telephone service built around speech recognition technology. Someone you know probably owns a Ford car that uses the SYNC system.

Making Progress

With all of these amazing uses of speech recognition systems around us, it is important to remind ourselves that the technology is still evolving. It is still far from perfect, as anyone who has used an automated telephone system will tell you. However, most voice recognition systems still manage to understand between 85 and 97 percent of words and phrases. Thirty years ago, they managed less than 50 percent. How quickly will they get to 100 percent?

Eventually all cars will be self-driving, allowing their owners to relax or even sleep instead of driving.

With developments in AI and voice recognition, shopping in stores will become more interactive.

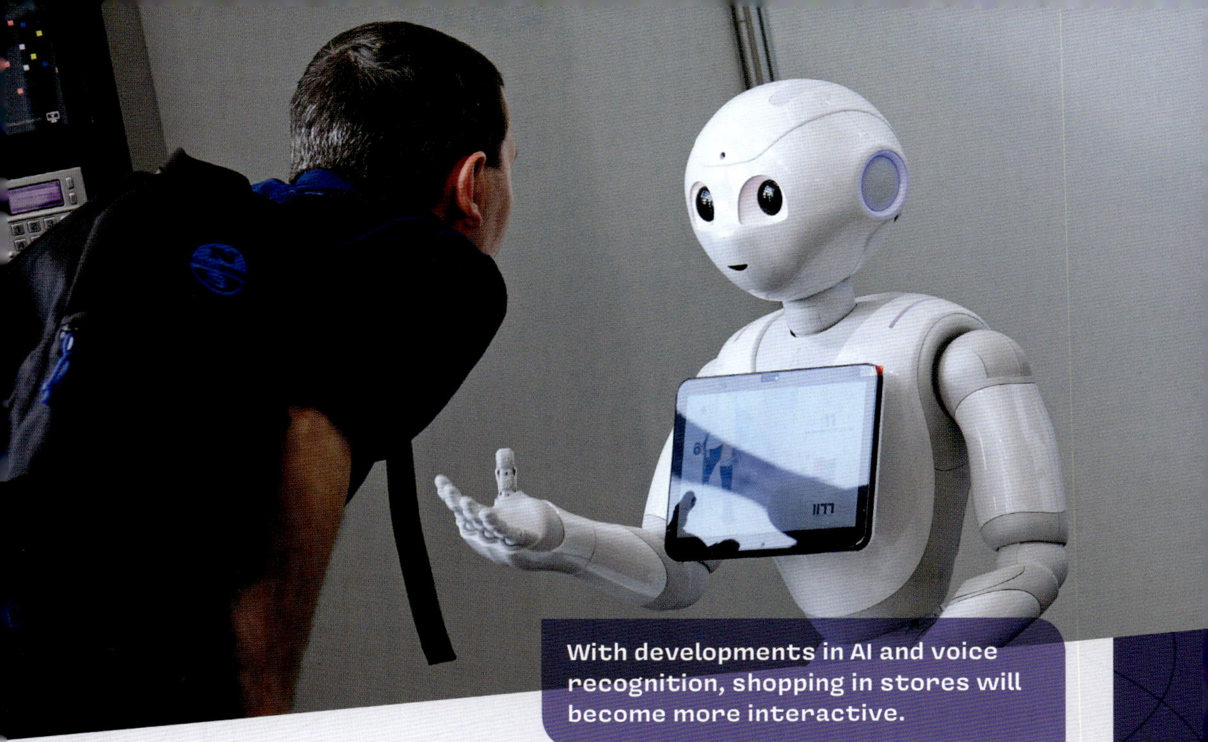

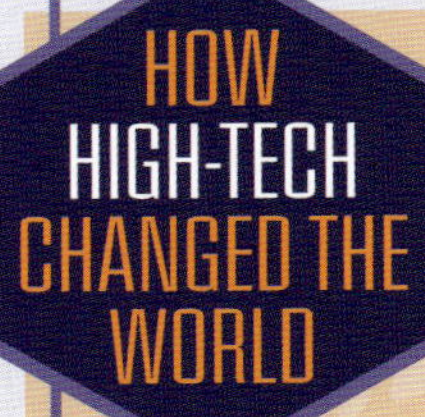

What's Next?

We can all imagine how speech recognition will change our lives in the future, from toilets that flush on command and earphones that instantly translate foreign languages to cars that drive themselves and robots that talk back to us. What do you think the future holds for voice recognition technology?

HOW HIGH-TECH CHANGED THE WORLD

Voice recognition technology can now understand when you speak in continuous sentences, as in a normal human conversation. It can now identify who you are and recognize your mood as you speak. Around one-quarter of Americans have a smart speaker AI assistant in their home, and more and more smartphone apps are including voice recognition. But one of the most exciting future developments will be in video games. Imagine future versions of Harry Potter or Spiderman games in which the player interacts with the nonplayer AI characters by holding a normal voice conversation with them!

GLOSSARY

algorithms sets of rules for solving a problem in a set number of steps

analog the opposite of digital. Sound waves are analog

artificial intelligence (AI) the ability of a machine to think and understand things like a human

automated designed to run with minimal human control, for example, automated telephone services

autonomous able to run without human control

biometrics identifying people by their characteristics, such as their voice or facial features

call centers offices where many operators man phones so that a company can deal with a large number of calls from customers

dictating speaking words to be recorded in writing

digital based on numbers

digital data information in a form that can be understood by digital devices such as computers

digitizing the process of turning sound, pictures, or movies into a digital file on a computer

interactive a two-way flow of information between a person and a machine, such as a robot

operating system the software included in computers, tablets, and smartphones that makes them work

phrase a sequence of two or more words that is not a fully formed sentence

pioneering done for the first time

probability how likely or possible it is that something will happen

prototype a first version of a device from which other forms are developed

regional accents differences in the way people speak according to where they live or were brought up

retired no longer working or in use

science-fiction a style of book, movie, or television series inspired by future technology and the wider universe

software an application on a computer designed for a specific purpose, for example, browsing the WWW or speech recognition

software engineer a scientist who writes or develops computer software programs

sound waves the vibrations created in the air by sounds

speech patterns unique variations in the way different people speak, for example, how quickly they talk, how they say certain words, and whether they have a regional accent

translates changes spoken or written words from one language to another

translator someone or something capable of translating spoken or written words from one language to another

word processing describes computer programs, such as Microsoft Word, that allow users to write documents

FIND OUT MORE

Books

Klepels, Alicia Z. *Artificial Intelligence and Humanoid Robots: 4D An Augmented Reading Experience* (The World of Artificial Intelligence 4D). Capstone, 2019.

Musolf, Nell. *Google* (Odysseys in Business). Creative Education, 2024.

Oxlade, Chris. *Computer Science for Curious Kids: An Illustrated Introduction to Software Programming, Artificial Intelligence, Cyber-Security—and More!* Arcturus, 2023.

Websites

Find out more about Honda's ASIMO and how it paved the way for other androids with voice recognition capabilities at:
https://global.honda/en/robotics

Learn more about Siri at:
https://kids.kiddle.co/Siri

Discover more about voice recognition at:
https://kids.kiddle.co/Speech_recognition

Publisher's note to educators and parents:
All the websites featured above have been carefully reviewed to ensure that they are suitable for students. However, many websites change often, and we cannot guarantee that a site's future contents will continue to meet our high standards of educational value. Please be advised that students should be closely monitored whenever they access the Internet.

INDEX

ABOUT THE AUTHOR

Kelly Roberts has written many children's science and technology books. Researching and writing this book has helped her learn more about voice activated technology and how this amazing tool has changed our world.